BIKING THE EMPIRE STATE TRAIL

A GUIDED TOUR FROM BUFFALO TO ALBANY

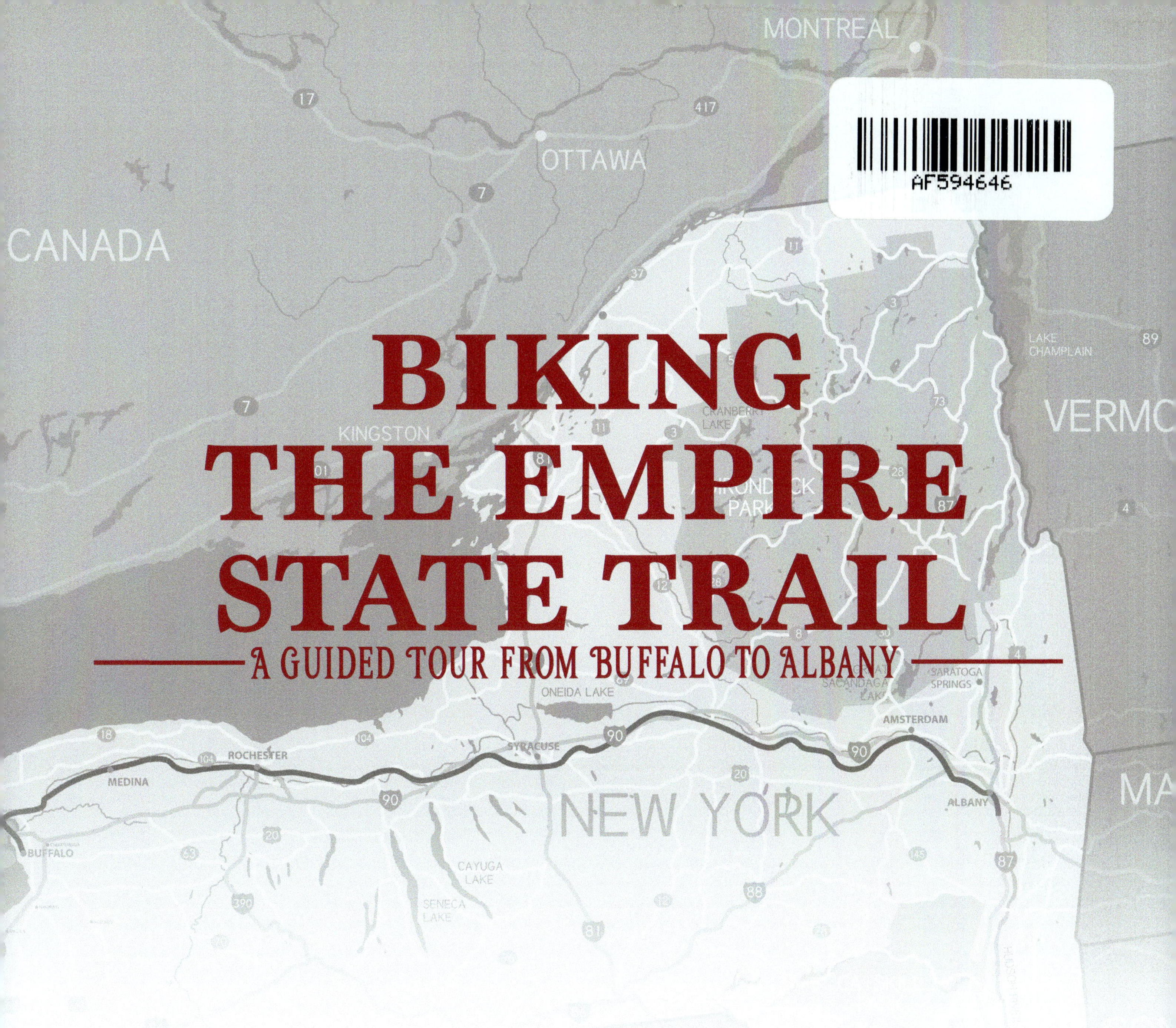

Written by Jennifer Hillman
and William McKeever
Photographs by Courtney Grim

Reedy Press
PO Box 5131
St. Louis, MO 63139
reedypress.com

Design: Richard Roden

ISBN: 9781681065779

Printed in the United States

25 26 27 28 29 5 4 3 2 1

DEDICATION

For those like-minded explorers who appreciate the journey and the many stops along the way.

BIKE SPOKES
COURTESY OF COURTNEY GRIM

WELL-MARKED SIGNAGE IS A HALLMARK OF THE ERIE CANALWAY AND EMPIRE STATE TRAIL SYSTEM. COURTESY OF COURTNEY GRIM

TABLE OF CONTENTS

CANAL BOAT AT SPENCERPORT
COURTESY OF WILLIAM MCKEEVER

ACKNOWLEDGMENTS

A book like this takes time and dedication to research, fact-check, and photograph and is only possible with the support of others.

In particular, thank you, Courtney Grim, for inspiring us to "take the ride" and for joining us on this 360-mile journey as our support car, emergency ride, and photographer. Once again, your photos show how beautiful New York State is and will inspire others to take the ride.

A special thank-you to Ashley Quimby-Simoni and Jean Mackay from the Erie Canalway National Heritage Corridor for your help and support.

And a big thanks to the Erie Canal Corporation and the citizens and government of New York State for creating, collaborating, and maintaining the 750-mile Empire State Trail system and the extraordinary free resources that are available on **empiretrail.ny.gov**. Thanks also to the many people we met, sharing the trail as we went along, as well as the residents and businesses of the communities we passed through.

As residents of Western New York, the authors of this guide are surrounded by the history of the Erie Canal. We decided to take the ride because we love adventures we can take at our own pace. We embrace the notion of slow travel with many stops along the way for little doses of history or to watch a turtle cross our path, identify an interesting wildflower with an internet app, or enjoy a refreshing ice cream or a great burger and cold beer.

We hope this book inspires you to bike, walk, run, roll, or paddle at your own pace along the Empire State Trail.

Take the ride and join an Erie Canal Challenge; learn more at eriecanalway.org/explore/challenge

WATERFORD HARBOR OVERLOOK
COURTESY OF ERIE CANALWAY NATIONAL HERITAGE CORRIDOR

FOREWORD

By Jean Mackay, Deputy Director of the Erie Canalway National Heritage Corridor

Two hundred years ago, the Erie Canal was boldly built to fuel America's expansion. Through remarkable vision, innovation, perseverance, and unforgiving work, this extraordinary waterway connected the Atlantic Ocean to the Great Lakes. Goods, people, and ideas flowed through its waters while cities rose along its banks, transforming New York State and our country forever.

Today, the Erie Canal continues to serve as the longest continuously operating canal system in North America. You can still take a boat "from Albany to Buffalo," as the Erie Canal song of old goes. But today's travelers do so on tour boats, vacation rentals, cruisers, and kayaks; bicycles have replaced mules on the former towpath. Designated as a National Historic Landmark in 2016, New York's canal system offers unparalleled opportunities to recreate with family and friends while discovering the incredible history and beauty of America's most famous human-made waterway.

Whether you like to cycle, hike, run, or roll, the Empire State Trail welcomes people of all abilities, from all walks of life and all backgrounds. The trail is both accessible and varied, so you can head out with friends or family for a few miles, enjoy a full day's journey to see the sights, or have an unforgettable multiday adventure. Lodging, dining, and visitor services are readily available short distances off the trail.

I made my first cycling trips along the Erie Canal back in 2005, taking my then fourth-grade son and his friends to ride their bikes for a few miles to experience the history that they were learning in school. By seventh grade, we ventured to central and western New York for longer weekend trips along the trail. In 2010, we geared up for a big adventure when we joined the 400-mile Cycling the Erie Canal cross-state bike tour from Buffalo to Albany.

Cycling the trail gave us a glimpse of what walking the towpath in the 1800s with mules and a boat in tow might have been like. We faced heat, rain, and slow going at times, but it taught us perseverance and appreciation for a hot shower at the end of the day. Rolling into towns along the way provided a sense of discovery as we sampled new foods

WEEDSPORT CANALWAY TRAIL
COURTESY OF ERIE CANALWAY
NATIONAL HERITAGE CORRIDOR

and local ice cream, poked through unique shops, and watched the Erie's famous lift bridges and locks in action. Each trip had its highs and lows, but the sense of discovery and accomplishment were beyond comparison.

I've since cycled more than 1,000 miles on the Empire State Trail, and each time feels both familiar and new. I love seeing all types of boats on the canal and exchanging a friendly wave as we pass. I love connecting with the people and places that preserve and share New York's extraordinary canal history. Their passion and dedication are inspiring. And I love being treated to genuine hometown hospitality in towns and villages that have welcomed canal travelers for 200 years.

You will, too. Let this guide spark your interest and set you on a path to cycling exploration along the Erie Canal. Plan to spend time on and off your bike. Towns along the trail are about 10 miles apart, so poke around when you reach one. Choose a museum or historic site to visit and enjoy a meal or treat before cycling to the next destination.

New York's mighty Empire State Trail is packed with history, beauty, and adventure. Get out and enjoy it. Mile after mile, you're in for an unforgettable journey.

INTRODUCTION

Traveling the Erie Canalway Trail on the Empire State Trail

The Erie Canalway Trail closely follows the 363-mile channel the original Erie Canal took from Buffalo to Albany. The overall Empire State Trail is a multiuse trail system 750 miles long and includes the Champlain Valley Trail heading north to Rouses Point at the Canada border and the Hudson Valley Greenway Trail heading south to New York City.

Today, just like in the past, a day on the Erie Canalway Trail will find you passing through farmlands, exploring quaint canal towns, and weaving through the bustling cities of Buffalo, Rochester, Syracuse, Rome, Amsterdam, and Albany.

How To Use This Book

The book is set up to encourage region-specific itineraries that can be enjoyed for either a few hours at a time or a few days in one region. It can be used by end-to-end cyclists as a supplemental resource to what you'll find at **empiretrail.ny.gov**.

Each major region is a section in the book. We highlight interesting stops within the region that are historic, fun and entertaining, or tasty, or that feature unique and beautiful scenery.

Each section will begin with the total end-to-end distance, a few highlights you can expect to see, and helpful usage icons.

WALL PAINTING AT CANASTOTA
COURTESY OF COURTNEY GRIM

Plan your outing based on your preferences for the level of difficulty and trail distance. The level of difficulty is a simple scale of easy, moderate, and difficult. Choose rides that match your experience and the experience of those accompanying you.

Biking safety, preparation, and suggested gear: The rides in this guide feature different kinds of experiences but are mostly flat, easy, and suitable for people of all abilities to bike, hike, run, or roll on the trail. We note any sections that are on-road or have significant elevation.

Wear a helmet —always!

Cotton kills. Cotton is great when you get off the trail. It's soft and feels lovely next to your skin. But on the trail, it holds in moisture from sweat and rain. When biking, layer your clothes and keep polyester (not nylon) next to your skin.

Leave word. Tell someone you're going biking, where you're going, and when you expect to be back.

Bring a bag. Always carry the following essentials with you:

- **Navigation:** Map and GPS-enabled device
- **Sun protection:** Sunglasses, sunscreen, and hat
- **Insulation:** Jacket, hat, gloves, rain shell, and thermal underwear
- **Illumination:** Flashlight, lanterns, and headlamp
- **First aid kit:** Buy a premade kit and modify/replace supplies as needed
- **Tools:** Bike pump, multi-tool, patch kit
- **Nutrition:** High-energy food that's easy to digest
- **Hydration:** Water
- **Bug spray**

Logistics

Most long-distance cyclists choose a west-to-east trip route, which we follow in this guide. Most of the trail has a slight downhill grade heading east. Cycling east also means more favorable winds—usually.

Trail Markers

The trail is well marked, and you'll often see the Empire State Trail marker alongside the Erie Canalway trail marker as they share the same path.

Planning Your Trip

When biking on a one-way trip, you have a few options:

- A two-car system of having a car at the start and end points
- A one-car system with a support driver to handle drop-off/pickup
- A one-car system with Amtrak and a major city. This option is available for itineraries in Buffalo, Rochester, Syracuse, and Albany. Amtrak allows carry-on bikes.
- End-to-ender. This requires knowing your daily travel distance and planning accommodations and/or camping along the way.
- Supported rides, such as the eight-day annual Parks & Trails New York—Cycle the Erie Canal ride, which is 40 to 60 miles a day
- Use empiretrail.ny.gov for up-to-date trail closures, conditions, lodging, and elevation details.

Now go on and take the ride.

Usage Icons:

Bathroom

Boat Rental

Bike Rental

Bike Repair Station

Camping

EV Charging Station

Food

Kayak Rental

Lodging

Paddling

No Services

Water

Wheeled Visitor Friendly

Trail Surface:

Gravel | Paved | Hard Pack | On-Road

Difficulty:

Easy (flat and off-road),
Moderate (mostly flat, off-road)

Medina Waterfalls and Culvert
Medina
Flight of Five Locks
Lockport
Gateway Harbor
Tonawanda
Buffalo
Outer Harbor/ Canalside
MONTREAL
ONEIDA LAKE
ROCHESTER
MEDINA
BUFFALO
SYRACUSE
AMSTERDAM
ALBANY
NEW YORK
CAYUGA LAKE
SENECA LAKE
GREAT SACANDAGA LAKE
SARATOGA SPRINGS
CATSKILL PARK
HUDSON RIVER

RIDE ONE

FLAT AND FABULOUS!

THE 50 MUST-SEE MILES OF THE ERIE CANAL

Western Route: Buffalo to Medina **Total Miles: 51.2**

What to Expect:

- Buffalo Outer Harbor and Canalside have enough activities for a two- to three-day visit.
- The ride is mostly off-road, paved, and level. There are small sections that weave through downtown Buffalo and the Tonawanda-Amherst areas.
- Exceptional scenery along Lake Erie, the Niagara River, and into the Erie Canal shows the historical significance of the western and current terminus of the Erie Canal and provides context on the economic impact the Erie Canal has had in this region.
- The local food scene is incredible; stop for small bites along each leg of this journey!
- A nice side excursion is to ride the Shoreline Trail from Tonawanda to Niagara Falls State Park; this 15-mile excursion follows the Niagara River to the iconic and mighty falls.

Begin at Buffalo's Small Boat Harbor and head two miles east on the trail.

Buffalo Outer Harbor

Starting at the Port of Buffalo Small Boat Harbor, cycle north along the eastern end of Lake Erie as it tapers into the upper Niagara River. This paved, flat trail weaves through Buffalo's industrial heritage areas, including several historic grain elevators—invented in Buffalo in 1842 by Joseph Dart, a merchant, and Robert Dunbar, an engineer.

Dart and Dunbar invented a marine grain elevator in which loose grain, scooped out by hand from the hulls of ships, is elevated to the top of a marine tower. Working examples can be viewed—and even smelled! The General Mills plant cooks up fragrant Cheerios and Fruit Loops daily, inspiring cereal cravings in all who roll by.

Stop by for a cold drink or meal at RiverWorks Sports, Adventure & Music Venue if time allows. This entertainment complex has options for the entire family, from kayak and paddleboard rentals to zip-lining, live music, and more. Keep an eye out for its colorfully lit Ferris wheel!

Usage Icons:

Trail Surface: Paved
Difficulty: Easy

From the trail, take the Queen City Bike Ferry ($1 each way) located at the end of Fuhrmann Boulevard to cross the Buffalo River to Canalside or park at Buffalo Canalside.

INDUSTRIAL HERITAGE BIKE TRAIL ALONG THE BUFFALO OUTER HARBOR
COURTESY OF WILLIAM MCKEEVER

SENECA CHIEF PACKET BOAT AT BUFFALO'S CANALSIDE
COURTESY OF COURTNEY GRIM

Buffalo Canalside

A must-see visit is the 1825 western terminus of the Erie Canal within the vibrant entertainment district of Canalside. An entire day could be spent enjoying concerts and festivals, outdoor fitness classes, the Explore and More Children's Museum, the Buffalo and Erie County Naval & Military Park, restaurants, and land or water history tours.

In the summer, the Queen City Bike Ferry takes pedestrians and cyclists on short one-way trips across the Buffalo River for a dollar. The south side of the river opens up your biking adventure to the entire Lake Erie Outer Harbor waterfront, including Wilkeson Pointe, Lakeside Bike Park, and Lakeside Complex with bike rentals, walking and cycling trails. North of the river there are plenty of local food trucks, restaurants, and picnic areas throughout Canalside and the Lake Erie Outer Harbor where you can enjoy Buffalo specialties like chicken wings, beef on weck, and local craft beer, as well as burgers and ice cream.

DID YOU KNOW?

Completed in 2024, the replica of the 1825 *Seneca Chief* packet boat can be viewed at the Buffalo Maritime Center. The original vessel transported Governor DeWitt Clinton and a bottle of Lake Erie water from Buffalo to New York City to mark the official opening of the Erie Canal.

Usage Icons:

Trail Surface: Paved
Difficulty: Easy

Continue east along the Shoreline/Canalway Trail for eight miles.

Tonawanda, Isleview Park

This 39-acre linear park is a local and regional magnet for boaters, anglers, birders, cyclists, walkers, sunny-day picnickers, and people-watchers. Overlooking the Niagara River and located on the Shoreline Trail between Buffalo and Amherst, the park is a great entryway to the Empire State Trail to travel either west toward Buffalo or east toward Amherst and Medina.

A ride through Isleview Park is not complete without stopping for a hot dog and ice cream at one of the old-time stands along Niagara Street, Tonawanda.

Usage Icons:

Trail Surface: Paved
Difficulty: Easy

Continue east along the Shoreline/Canalway Trail for 2.5 miles.

Tonawanda, Gateway Harbor

The western entrance to the current Erie Canalway, the twin cities of Tonawanda and North Tonawanda are two distinct cities, in separate counties, bisected yet joined culturally by the historic Erie Canal. These charming and historic canal towns continue to thrive as a destination for shopping, dining, boating, cycling, music festivals, and just hanging out.

Summer music festivals and Canalfest of the Tonawandas are signature events that draw hundreds of thousands of visitors. The restored and historic Riviera Theatre, built in 1926, thrives today and draws national music, dance, and comedy acts.

Usage Icons:

Trail Surface: Paved
Difficulty: Easy

GATEWAY PARK IN TONAWANDA AT CANAL DAYS
COURTESY OF COURTNEY GRIM

LOCKPORT FLIGHT OF FIVE LOCKS
COURTESY OF COURTNEY GRIM

Continue east along the Canalway Trail for 19.7 miles.

Lockport: The Flight of Five Locks

Famous and iconic, the Flight of Five Locks is an Erie Canal engineering marvel with a total lift of 49 feet. Located in the Lockport Locks District, Locks 69 and 70 were originally completed in 1849 and have been recently restored. Today, you can see the lock's massive wooden gates, operated by hand, next to the modern Locks 34 and 35.

Canal Street, a pedestrian and bicycle-only street overlooking the locks, is a bustling, revitalized canal town; highlights are the Erie Canal Discovery Center, Lake Effect Ice Cream, Flight of Five Winery, and the Lockport Caves and Underground Boat Rides. A must on your Empire State Trail to-do list is to take a boat cruise through the Lockport Locks and Erie Canal Cruises to "elevate" your experience!

DID YOU KNOW?

The Flight of Five Locks is a staircase lock constructed to lift or lower a canal boat over the 49-foot-high Niagara Escarpment. As the upper side goes down, the lower side comes up.

Usage Icons:

Trail Surface: Paved
Difficulty: Easy

Continue east along the Canalway Trail for 16.8 miles.

Medina—Waterfalls, Aqueducts, and Culverts

This quaint canal town is famous for its handsome red-brown sandstone deposits aptly named "Medina Sandstone," which was shipped around the world for nearly 150 years. It can be seen as a building material for houses along Route 104 in Niagara and Orleans Counties.

The trail passes over the Medina Waterfall; technically, this is an aqueduct from Oak Orchard Creek and passes under the Erie Canal. Two miles west on the trail is the Medina Culvert, the only spot on the Erie Canal where you can drive a car under the canal!

Medina is also in the agricultural belt, where you can enjoy fresh-picked summer and fall produce. A favorite stop of ours, slightly off the trail, is the emerging cluster of Mexican restaurants, including Mariachi de Oro, serving local produce paired with authentic Mexican cuisine.

Usage Icons:

Trail Surface: Gravel
Difficulty: Easy

MEDINA CULVERT GOES UNDER THE ERIE CANAL
COURTESY OF COURTNEY GRIM

MONTREAL
Medina
Brockport
Spencerport
Rochester
Genessee
Valley Park
Pittsford
& Lock 32
Fairport
ONEIDA LAKE
ROCHESTER
MEDINA
BUFFALO
SYRACUSE
AMSTERDAM
ALBANY
NEW YORK
CAYUGA
LAKE
SENECA
LAKE
GREAT
SACANDAGA
LAKE
SARATOGA
SPRINGS
CATSKILL
PARK
HUDSON RIVER

RIDE TWO

QUAINT COUNTRYSIDES AND HISTORIC CANAL TOWNS

Western Route: Medina to Fairport **Total Miles: 58.3**

PARK AVENUE LIFT BRIDGE IN BROCKPORT
COURTESY OF WILLIAM MCKEEVER

What to Expect:

- The ride from Medina to Brockport is mostly in the sun through farmland with limited services; bring your water, snacks, and sun protection.
- Albion is a nice stopover from Medina to Brockport for a cold drink, ice cream, and a stretch.
- Try to build in time for a side excursion along the Genesee River Trail. This 90-mile trail goes from the Erie Canal to Lake Ontario.
- Visit Old Erie Canal Lock 62 behind the Pittsford Plaza to see a well-preserved lock.
- Stop and watch one of the historic lift bridges of Rochester in action in Adams Basin, Spencerport, or Fairport.

Start at the Welcome Center at 11 Water Street, Brockport, and head east along the Canalway Trail.

The Bridge to Brockport

Dug through the top of the Medina Escarpment, the Erie Canal traverses Brockport with the land dropping off sharply northward toward Lake

Ontario, 250 feet lower. The land southward is 200 feet higher because of the Niagara Escarpment.

Brockport, known as the Victorian Village on the Erie Canal, is a quaint canal village in Rochester that features a 100-year-old lift bridge recently restored for reopening in 2025 to mark the Erie Canal's Bicentennial. Visit the Brockport Canal Landing; this public park hosts many canal-centric events, including the Low Bridge High Water Festival celebrating the opening of the Erie Canal navigation season. Clustered around the Landing you'll find several shops and restaurants to explore, including the Brockport Welcome Center.

Usage Icons:

Trail Surface: Gravel | Hard Pack
Difficulty: Easy

Continue east on the Canalway Trail for 7.7 miles.

Spencerport Depot & Canal Museum

A stop at the Spencerport Depot & Canal Museum is a nice diversion and offers exhibits and displays about the Erie Canal and local history. The museum has a welcome center, restrooms, a bike rack, and a gift shop.

Within walking distance are shops, restaurants, and fishing spots. Spencerport hosts Canal Days on the last weekend of July each year with food tents, arts and crafts vendors, and music. During the summer you can catch the free Music on the Canal Concert Series each Sunday evening.

SPENCERPORT DEPOT
COURTESY OF WILLIAM MCKEEVER

Usage Icons:

Trail Surface: Gravel | Paved
Difficulty: Easy

Continue east on the Canalway Trail for 12 miles.

Genesee Valley Park, Where Waters Meet

Three waterways—the Erie Canal, Red Creek, and the Genesee River—all intersect in this Frederick Law Olmsted park designed and originally called "South Park." This 800-acre park has stunning rolling hills, wooded paths, and bridges over and along the three waterways.

It's a lovely place to wander around, picnic, and appreciate the changes this land has seen. The Genesee River served as a border between the lands of the Seneca and Erie Indigenous peoples. The name *Genesee* comes from the Seneca and means "beautiful or pleasant valley."

TIP! Pay attention to trail markers here, as the Genesee Greenway Trail heads north into the city and the Canalway Trail/Empire State Trail continues east.

Usage Icons:

Trail Surface: Gravel | Paved
Difficulty: Moderate

GENESEE VALLEY PARK IN ROCHESTER
COURTESY OF WILLIAM MCKEEVER

LOCK 32 WHITEWATER PARK
COURTESY OF KEITH BOAS

Continue east on the Canalway Trail for 6.4 miles to Lock 32 White Water Park. You can also park and start at the Erie Canal Heritage Trail, 12 Schoen Place, Pittsford.

Pittsford and Lock 32

Take a break and explore the Erie Canal from the water on a replica packet boat with Sam Patch Erie Canal Tours. The cruises depart from Schoen Place, located in the Port of Pittsford along with Lock 32 Brewing, a local favorite for great food, craft beer, and lively music and entertainment overlooking the canal.

Nearby is Lock 32 Paddling Center and Whitewater Park, where kayak and canoe rentals are available for both the flat water and white water sections of the Erie Canal.

Usage Icons:

Trail Surface: Gravel | Paved

Difficulty: Easy

Continue east on the Canalway Trail for 8.6 miles or park and start at the municipal parking lot.

Fairport Canal Front Promenade

The 1914 Fairport Lift Bridge slopes 32 degrees, giving the bridge an irregular shape with no two angles being the same. With this unique backdrop, the charming waterfront village is a beacon for locals and those exploring the canal on foot, pedaling, or paddling along the waterway.

At Fairport Harbor and Packetts Landing you can enjoy shopping, restaurants, and ice cream/gelato, as well as an Erie Canal cruise on the *Colonial Belle*. Rail fans can check out the train-viewing platform at Fairport Junction with a live audio feed from the trains. Fairport's annual Canal Days festival is held the first weekend in June each year with thousands of visitors sampling food and enjoying local artisans and live music.

DID YOU KNOW?

The Fairport Lift Bridge is "one of the Most Unusual Bridges in NYS" according to a 1976 Landmark Society survey because of its irregular shape and none of its angles being the same.

Usage Icons:

Trail Surface: Gravel | Paved

Difficulty: Easy

SCHOEN PLACE, PITTSFORD
COURTESY OF KEITH BOAS

MONTREAL
Syracuse
Camillus
EC Park
Centerport
Fairport
Lyons
Montezuma
NWR
Port
Byron
Onnondaga
Lake County
Park
Erie Canal
Museum
ONEIDA LAKE
ROCHESTER
MEDINA
BUFFALO
SYRACUSE
AMSTERDAM
ALBANY
NEW YORK
GREAT
SACANDAGA
LAKE
SARATOGA
SPRINGS
CAYUGA
LAKE
SENECA
LAKE
CATSKILL
PARK
HUDSON RIVER

RIDE THREE

WIDE WATERS, WOODS, AND WETLANDS

Central Route: Fairport to Syracuse **Total Miles: 80.5**

What to Expect:

- The trail from Clyde to Syracuse has long sections of on-road biking and rolling hills in several sections that can be difficult.
- Take a scenic side trip by bike or car from Clyde to Seneca Falls along the western edge of Seneca Lake. Pass by the Daniel Thorn Farm with more than one million sunflowers and on to the Women's Rights National Historic Park.
- The Empire State Trail travels along Onondaga Lake and through the New York State Fairgrounds, weaving through downtown Syracuse with plenty of stops along the way to grab an ice cream, cold drink, and some of Syracuse's claim-to-fame foods, like salt potatoes, Heid's Hotdogs, and Dinosaur Bar-B-Que.

Erie Canal Bike Trail parking is available at Abbey Park, 177 Water Street, Lyons, 0.4 mile west of the trail entrance. Head east on the trail.

Lyons: The Peppermint Village

In 1839, Hiram Gilbert Hotchkiss discovered wild peppermint growing and started working with local farmers to cultivate and distill it into oil. The proximity to the Erie Canal allowed the peppermint oil to be shipped internationally and gain recognition as the purest and best-tasting peppermint in the world, giving Lyon's the nickname of "The Peppermint Village."

H. G. Hotchkiss Essential Oil Company peppermint oils could be found in early medicinal products and in Beech-Nut gum. Howard Johnson, the large restaurant chain, was another major customer. Today you can visit the Peppermint Museum, which is located on the Erie Canal and Empire State Trail, or plan a trip during the annual Lyons Peppermint Days in July.

Usage Icons:

Trail Surface: On-Road

Difficulty: Moderate

THE PEPPERMINT VILLAGE
COURTESY OF ERIE CANALWAY NATIONAL HERITAGE CORRIDOR

MONTEZUMA NATIONAL WILDLIFE REFUGE
COURTESY OF COURTNEY GRIM

Continue east for 23 miles along the Canalway Trail.

Montezuma National Wildlife Refuge

A short distance off the Empire State Trail is the Montezuma Audubon Center in Savannah, with several flat and boardwalk trails along marshes and through open meadows, forests, and lakes. The 10,000-plus-acre refuge is located in one of the most active flight lanes in the Atlantic Flyway and is a refuge and breeding ground for migratory birds and other wildlife.

Frequent bird sightings include eagles, hawks, waterfowl, and shorebirds; there is also a live feed from an osprey nest-cam and a purple martin nest-cam. Note that bikes are permitted at the nature center, but not on the trails.

Usage Icons:

Trail Surface: Gravel

Difficulty: Easy

Continue east on the Canalway Trail for 11 miles.

Port Byron Old Erie Canal Heritage Park

Located along the New York State Thruway between exits 40 and 41, this park encourages visitors to walk through the impressively large stone structure of Lock 52, built in 1853, and tour the restored 1894 Erie House Tavern & Hotel, mule barn, and blacksmith shop. The volunteers operating the exhibits are passionate and knowledgeable about the area and its history.

TIP! If biking from the Empire State Trail to the park, you'll navigate local roads to get to the park.

Usage Icons:

Trail Surface: On-Road

Difficulty: Moderate

PORT BYRON AND ERIE CANAL MUSEUM
COURTESY OF COURTNEY GRIM

CENTREPORT AQUEDUCT PARK
COURTESY OF JENNIFER HILLMAN

Continue east on the Erie Canalway Trail for 3.1 miles.

Centreport Aqueduct Park

The Centreport Aqueduct, built in 1855, is the centerpiece of this small park. Built to carry the Erie Canal over the confluence of North Brook and Cold Springs Brook, this three-span stone-and-wood structure is one of the original 33 aqueducts built during the construction of the Erie Canal.

This aqueduct is unusual because the dam creates a pool of "dead" water above the aqueduct, allowing gravel and silt to settle out of the stream. The dam then creates a beautiful waterfall as it passes under the aqueduct.

Usage Icons:

Trail Surface: Gravel | Hard Pack

Difficulty: Easy

Head eastward for 16 miles on the Erie Canalway Trail.

Camillus Erie Canal Park

Take a boat tour on the Erie Canal over the famous Nine Mile Creek Aqueduct, built in 1841. The Sims

Store Museum is a fun experience, with exhibits, early photos, and maps of the canal with models of locks, aqueducts, and canal boats.

Outdoors there is a steam engine exhibit and over 13 miles of hiking and biking both on and off the Erie Canal Trail.

Usage Icons:

Trail Surface: Paved

Difficulty: Easy

CAMILLUS ERIE CANAL PARK
COURTESY OF JENNIFER HILLMAN

Continue east on the Erie Canalway Trail for 6.5 miles to the New York State Fairgrounds. Enter the fairgrounds from Bridge Street and cross the pedestrian bridge over the New York State Thruway. Head west along the lake shoreline until the trail splits, then turn right to head east along the southern/western lakeshore. Curving along the eastern end of the lake, the route traverses the linear park along the northern/eastern shore of the lake to the Salt Museum, approximately seven miles from the fairgrounds.

Onondaga Lake County Park and the Salt Museum

This eight-mile linear park is on the shores of Onondaga Lake and features several walking and biking trails, picnic areas, and Syracuse's Salt Museum, built on the site of an original salt boiling block. Nicknamed "Salt City," Syracuse was the nation's salt production capital in the mid-1800s. Salt was refined from concentrated salt brine springs at the southern end of Onondaga Lake. The Erie Canal provided an opportunity for shipping Syracuse Salt nationally.

DID YOU KNOW?

Salt potatoes, a Syracuse specialty, are said to have been created when the salt factory workers would drop potatoes in the boiling brine.

ONONDAGA LAKE COUNTY PARK
COURTESY OF JENNIFER HILLMAN

Usage Icons:

Trail Surface: Paved

Difficulty: Moderate

From Liverpool, double back heading eastward for 5.4 miles along the shoreline and then into downtown Syracuse.

Syracuse: Erie Canal Museum

Located in downtown Syracuse, the 1850 Syracuse Weighlock Building was originally built as a weigh station for boats traveling on the canal. Visitors to the museum can learn how boats entered a locked chamber and how measurements were calculated on the weight of the cargo. Boats were charged a toll based on their weight and travel distance.

Today the museum features exhibits on the history and construction of the canal. The museum's weigh chamber contains the Frank *Buchanan Thomson*, a full-size replica of a line boat that would have carried cargo and passengers on the canal.

Usage Icons:

Trail Surface: Paved | On-Road

Difficulty: Easy

MONTREAL
CAN
Church
Chittenango
Landing
Green
Lakes SP
DeWitt
Fort Herkimer
Canajorharie
Amsterdam
NEW YORK
LAKE
ONTARIO
ONEIDA LAKE
GREAT
SACANDAGA
LAKE
SARATOGA
SPRINGS
ROCHESTER
MEDINA
BUFFALO
SYRACUSE
AMSTERDAM
ALBANY
NEW YORK
CAYUGA
LAKE
SENECA
LAKE
CATSKILL
PARK
HUDSON RIVER

RIDE FOUR

CYCLE THROUGH HISTORY ON

OLD ERIE CANAL PARK TO MOHAWK VALLEY

Eastern Route: DeWitt to Amsterdam **Total Miles: 118**

What to Expect:

- Cycle the Old Erie Canal Park from DeWitt to Rome and hop on and off at the historic canal towns of DeWitt, Chittenango, Canastota, and Rome.
- Cycle over five historic aqueducts at DeWitt, Cedar Bay Picnic Area, Limestone Creek, Cowaselon Creek, and Oneida Creek.
- Stop for a paddle or hike at Green Lakes State Park, which features two glacial lakes that are great for swimming, paddling, or picnicking.
- Picnic and rest stops are plentiful at Cedar Bay, Green Lakes State Park, Poolsbrook Picnic Area, and Rome's Erie Canal Village.
- Must-stops are the Chittenango Landing Canal Boat Museum and the Canastota Canal Tow Museum.

Park at the Butternut Creek Erie Canal Trailhead on Butternut Drive, north of Kinne Road. Continue east through the park.

Old Erie Canal State Historic Park, DeWitt

This 36-mile linear park has several easy access points and is a delightful, flat, and easy ride on the original towpath alongside the remains of the historic Enlarged Erie Canal. In DeWitt you'll start your ride at the Butternut Creek Aqueduct and pass through Cedar Bay Picnic area. This trail is well-traveled and has beautiful canal views, historic stone locks, aqueducts, wetlands, and wildlife.

It's common to see dozens of turtles sunning themselves on floating logs during the warm days of summer and birds of prey soaring above. The trail itself is dotted with seasonal wildflowers, raspberries, and blackberries.

Whether you prefer to cycle, hike, run, or roll, this accessible linear park has interesting features that can provide a lovely, leisurely experience along the towpath for a few hours or an entire day.

Usage Icons:

Trail Surface: Paved | Hard Pack

Difficulty: Easy

OLD ERIE CANAL STATE PARK
COURTESY OF WILLIAM MCKEEVER

GREEN LAKES STATE PARK
COURTESY OF ERIE CANALWAY
NATIONAL HERITAGE CORRIDOR

Travel east on the Erie Canalway Trail for 12 miles.

Green Lakes State Park

The Empire State Trail is adjacent to Green Lakes State Park, and easy access to the park is available on a well-marked footbridge. There are 14 trails along the park; by far the most popular trail goes around the two glacial lakes that give the park its name.

These surreal, aquamarine glacial lakes likely formed at the end of the last ice age and feature an unusual geology as rare meromictic lakes, which means that the surface and bottom waters don't mix in the fall and spring. This phenomenon is due to the lakes' small surface areas and deep plunge pools that protect the water from wind.

The bottom water in the lakes is oxygen-deprived. This rare phenomenon only occurs in about 30 lakes worldwide, making the Green Lakes among the most studied lakes in the world for ancient plant and animal life.

DID YOU KNOW?

Green Lakes is home to rare freshwater "reefs" that are continually growing. At Deadman's Point, the large "reef" looks like coral, but it is made of millions of underwater microbes forming reef-like structures.

Usage Icons:

Trail Surface: Gravel | Paved

Difficulty: Easy

Continue east on the Erie Canalway Trail for 6.1 miles.

Chittenango Landing Canal Boat Museum

Experience canal life in this museum that literally has a boatload of history. Located on the historic site of the canal's 19th-century dry dock complex, this re-created canal village invites you to experience what life was like working and living along the Erie Canal.

The main feature is an excavated and preserved three-bay dry dock that 19th-century craftsmen used to build and repair canal boats from 1855 until the opening of the Barge Canal in 1918. Explore history with a visit to the reconstructed general store, which features a vast collection of artifacts belonging to the Chittenango site as well as the overall history of the Erie Canal.

The 27-acre property features several hands-on learning exhibits that entertain the entire family, including a working blacksmith shop, a boat shop, a mule stable, a sawmill, a walk-on canal boat, and the remains of a sunken canal boat.

Drive, bike, or paddle here; in the summer you can rent bikes and kayaks. Visit in early June for the annual Boat Float N' Folk Festival and join hundreds of other paddlers and visitors enjoying canal life with local food, music, and folk arts.

Usage Icons:

Trail Surface: Gravel | Paved

Difficulty: Easy

CHITTENANGO LANDING CANAL BOAT MUSEUM
COURTESY OF ERIE CANALWAY NATIONAL HERITAGE CORRIDOR

FORT HERKIMER CHURCH
COURTESY OF ERIE CANALWAY NATIONAL HERITAGE CORRIDOR

Continue east on the Erie Canalway Trail for 62 miles.

Fort Herkimer Church

Completed in 2020, this newer section of the Empire State Trail allows bikers to travel between Fort Herkimer and on to Little Falls on one off-road path. This section winds through rural areas and quaint canal towns, and it offers a quiet and enjoyable experience with stunning views of the Mohawk River.

Along the way, stop at the Fort Herkimer Church, built between 1753 and 1767. This is one of the oldest churches in New York State and the oldest building in Herkimer County. It has served the community not only as a church for early settlers, but also as a fortress during both the French and Indian War and the American Revolution.

DID YOU KNOW?

Herkimer is also known for its "diamond mines." Herkimer "diamonds" are double-terminated, faceted quartz of great clarity formed over 500 million years ago. You can try your luck at finding these gems by visiting one of the mines or wading through creekside gravel beds at several public access points along West Canada Creek.

Usage Icons:

Trail Surface: Gravel | Paved

Difficulty: Easy

Heading east on the Erie Canalway Trail, continue for 25 miles.

Canajoharie—Falls, Food, and Art

Cycling into Canajoharie from the east you'll pass over the Mohawk River and Erie Canal and descend into this quaint and vibrant town. The Empire State Trail weaves right through Canajoharie, past great old buildings with eclectic shops, welcoming restaurants, and plenty of green space for stretching your legs and walking about.

You could easily while away the day in this historic village by visiting Wintergreen Park and Canajoharie Falls, checking out the Arkel Museum, and tasting your way through town at the local establishments. The name Canajoharie comes from the Mohawk name *Can-a-jor-ha*, which means the "pot that washes itself." This was given because its namesake creek has a naturally occurring "pothole" about 20 feet in diameter and about 10 feet deep at the base of the falls. You can take an easy one-mile round-trip hike to the 45-foot waterfall.

The Arkel Museum has an extensive collection of American art depicting the history of the Mohawk River Valley and Erie Canal.

Usage Icons:

Trail Surface: Gravel | Paved

Difficulty: Easy

Continue on the Canalway Trail east for 22 miles.

CANAJOHARIE FALLS AND POTHOLE
COURTESY OF PARKS & TRAILS NEW YORK

MONTREAL
Amsterdam
Schenectady
Cohoes
Falls
Albany
NEW YORK
AMSTERDAM
ALBANY
ROCHESTER
SYRACUSE
BUFFALO
MEDINA
GREAT
SACANDAGA
LAKE
SARATOGA
SPRINGS
CAYUGA
LAKE
SENECA
LAKE
CATSKILL
PARK
HUDSON RIVER

RIDE FIVE

MOHAWK VALLEY TO THE CAPITAL REGION

Eastern Route: Amsterdam to Albany **Total Miles: 46.8**

What to Expect:

- This section can easily be done in a day if you are focused; however, there is so much to appreciate and explore we recommend two to three days.
- The Mohawk–Hudson bike trail from Amsterdam to Schenectady is a paved and winding off-road path through woods, wetlands, and farmlands, with stunning Mohawk River views and rest stops.
- As you cycle through downtown Schenectady, the trail goes through Little Italy. Be sure to stop for sweet or savory treats!
- Cohoes Falls is the second-largest waterfall in New York State after Niagara Falls and is truly a hidden gem of the Capital region.
- Stop and check out Canal Locks E10 and E8.

Begin at the Little Italy Gateway at North Jay and Union Streets. Continue along the trail.

Amsterdam and the Mohawk Valley Gateway Overlook Pedestrian Bridge

The "Park over the River" spans 511 feet over the north and south banks of the Mohawk River in curved, natural shapes and has 12 points along the path that tell the history of the Mohawk Valley and its peoples. Completed in 2016, the park celebrates and connects the past, present, and future of transportation and industries that rely on the canal, railroad, and roads, including farming, water power, and factories.

DID YOU KNOW?

Amsterdam had the largest pearl button factory in the world. In 1912, Arthur Chalmer's Hampshire Pearl Button Factory produced over $1.5 million worth of buttons annually. They were so plentiful that the Jollyland amusement park paved sidewalks with discarded buttons.

As the Empire State Trail enters East Amsterdam from Canajoharie, the first trailhead shares the parking lot with Lorenzo's Southside, a local Italian restaurant with a great bar and even better pizza. Be sure to stop in for a cold drink and great local food before heading onto the next stop.

Usage Icons:

Trail Surface: Gravel | Paved

Difficulty: Easy

WHEEL OF LIFE MOSIAC AT THE MOHAWK VALLEY GATEWAY OVERLOOK BRIDGE IN AMSTERDAM
PHOTO COURTESY OF CITY OF AMSTERDAM

Schenectady's Historic Stockade District and Little Italy

Heading east into downtown Schenectady, the trail is mostly off-road except for a short, delightful three-quarter-mile section that guides you through the Stockade District and Little Italy.

The Stockade District dates back 300 years and is one of the oldest neighborhoods in America. The trail invites you to explore the sights, sounds, and delicious smells as you roll past more than 400 historic homes dating back 200-plus years.

As you head under the Little Italy entrance gateway, you'll discover several iconic Italian cafès, bars, and restaurants that are welcoming and bike-friendly. Be sure to stop into one of these local establishments for coffee and pastry or a more relaxing meal.

DID YOU KNOW?

Thomas Edison founded what would become General Electric and George Westinghouse invented the rotary engine and air brakes in Schenectady.

Usage Icons:

Trail Surface: Paved

Difficulty: Easy

SCHENECTADY HISTORIC STOCKADE DISTRICT AND LITTLE ITALY
COURTESY OF WILLIAM MCKEEVER

COHOES FALLS IN COHOES, NEW YORK
COURTESY OF COURTNEY GRIM

Head eastward 19 miles on the Erie Canalway Trail.

Cohoes Falls and Overlook Park

Towering 90 feet high and 1,000 feet across is the second-largest cataract in New York State, Cohoes Falls. The earliest reference to the falls is in the oral histories of the Mohawk tribe, where it is called *Ga-ha'oose*, meaning "the place of the falling canoe."

Cohoes Falls was a major obstacle to boat transportation on the Mohawk River, but as Europeans settled into the area, it was also recognized as a potential source of water power. In 1826, the Cohoes Company formed and shortly after built the first dam above the falls along with two bypass canals in 1831. This first dam was destroyed in an ice floe, and a new stone-and-concrete dam was built in 1839.

In 1825, as the Erie Canal was being built through Cohoes, engineers created a 16-lock bypass around the falls. These locks were called the "terrible sixteens" because it took a full day to navigate through the 16 locks.

TIP! When reaching Cohoes from the west, turn left on Manor Avenue. You will leave the trail and ride on city streets for the last quarter mile. Turn right on Mohawk Street to reach Cohoes Falls.

Usage Icons:

Trail Surface: Paved
Difficulty: Easy

Continue east for 2.4 miles on the Erie Canalway Trail.

Peebles Island State Park

Nestled at the confluence of the Mohawk and Hudson Rivers, Peebles Island has a long and rich history dating back thousands of years, with the Mohican tribe occupying the Hudson River Valley until the 1600s.

Henry Hudson's ship, the *Half Moon*, sent a small boat up what is now known as the Hudson River documenting the island in 1609. The island's location gave it strategic importance in the Revolutionary War, with a British fort built across the river (in today's Waterford), and a Continental Army encampment built in 1777 to engage the British Army heading south from Montreal. Remains of this encampment still exist today.

When you visit the island you can see the remains of the Matton Shipyard, established in 1916, which built more than 300 vessels, including tugboats, police boats, canal boats, barges, and World War II submarine chasers.

For those biking through the area, this is a nice location to rest or stretch your legs and pick up a bite to eat in either Waterford or Green Island. The 190-acre park has stunning views and a trail that circles the island. While you can bike to Peebles Island, bicycles are not allowed on the island's trails. Hiking only! To get there, you'll bike on city streets with bike lanes.

Usage Icons:

Trail Surface: Paved

Difficulty: Easy

BRIDGE TO PEEBLES LANDING
COURTESY OF WILLIAM MCKEEVER

DID YOU KNOW?

Peebles Island State Park is not just a confluence of rivers, but also a confluence of bike trails. From here you can go north through Waterford to Whitehall and continue to the Champlain Trail, which extends 110 miles to the American–Canadian border at Rouses Point, New York.

Follow the Canalway Trail eastward for 10 miles.

Jennings Landing at the Corning Preserve

The official end of the east-to-west Empire State Trail is at Corning Preserve and Jennings Landing. This city park was once the Albany Basin and the eastern terminus of the Erie Canal. Constructed and completed in 1825 as a protected canal, the Albany Basin wooden pier and wharves extended over one mile and provided safe harbor for 1,000 canal boats and 50 larger vessels—each day.

Today, Jennings Landing remains a gathering place with trails, boat launch sites, and beautiful views of the Hudson River. In the summer the park hosts concerts at the 1,000-person amphitheater and provides access to downtown Albany across a pedestrian bridge.

DID YOU KNOW?

From Jennings Landing you can continue south on the Hudson Valley Greenway Trail 200 miles to Battery Park at the southern tip of Manhattan. This trail is mainly off-road as it meanders through the Hudson River Valley with some occasional on-road spots.

Usage Icons:

Trail Surface: Paved

Difficulty: Easy

JENN AND BILL FINISHING IN ALBANY
COURTESY OF COURTNEY GRIM

INDEX